WALK

WITH

SPIRIT

BY

SUSAN THOMAS

UNDERWOOD *from NW*

A Native American approach to
SPIRITUALITY

Produced in association with the

North Woods Press
Conservatory of American Letters
P.O. Box 298, Thomaston ME. 04861

Walk With Spirit

Copyright 1998 by Susan Thomas Underwood
All rights reserved. Limited 1st edition 1100 s&n.
2nd printing 2001, 3rd printing 2005, 4th printing 2007.

Library of Congress Cataloging-in-Publication Data

Underwood, Susan Thomas, 1950-
Walk With Spirit / Susan Thomas
Underwood

ISBN #0-89002-340-9

Library of Congress Catalogue Card number:
#98-90389

Printed in the United States of America

Copies of this publication may be purchased by writing Underwood Studio at the above address.

About the cover painting
The Healer

Losing a husband to kidney cancer in 1991 while under the care of medical doctors, the artist now studies techniques of spiritual healing. This vision came to the artist when she was most diligent in these studies. Nearing completion of the painting and searching for its name, she came upon American Indian literature identifying the wolf as the sign of the healer. Amazed at the connection to the circumstances surrounding her vision, Susan had the perfect name for her painting.

This wolf materialized in the artist' life in 1996 when a couple seeking a country home for their wolf asked Susan to take him to her ranch. There *Usdi Waya* (Little Wolf) dwells happily at the time of this printing in 1998. He is pictured with the artist/author on the back cover.

In 1997, Susan's mother was diagnosed with kidney cancer and died 4 short months later. Usdi served his title well as he lended comfort and healing that only a four-legged can give.

DEDICATION

I wish to dedicate this book to my ancestors (including my father) from whom I received my Native American blood and Shawnee heritage; and to my Native American tribe, friends, and teachers who have shared so freely.

Introduction

I am a native born Oklahoman and, as many of my fellows within this state, have flowing within me the blood of an Indian tribe. As our American society is a mixture of many races, cultures and religions, I am a product of Oklahoma's former years as *Indian Territory*; a place set aside for Indian tribes after removal from homelands across most of the United States. Indian Territory lasted under 100 years, as pressure for white settlement caused our government to make the territory into a state.

I am a member of the Loyal Band of Shawnee, a band that fought with our great chief, Tecumseh for homelands in Ohio until his death and the near extinction of our band. I am not, however; a full-blooded Shawnee, and do not claim to represent the views or beliefs of my tribe or any other Indian tribe. I am also German, Scotch-Irish, and English, and was influenced by these cultures also.

My Shawnee blood comes from my father. Upon his Indian mother's death when he was 6 years old, he was placed in an orphanage and had no significant contact with his family again. My mother was white, and I was raised white. My Indian blood began to pull at me during the cancer illness and death of my first husband. Through this trial, the Indian side of me seemed to surface, blossom, and finally, to dominate.

Today, I live Indian. It seems that with my mother's death, I lost my last bond to white culture. My knowledge of Indian culture has come from my Shawnee tribesmen, a Lakota wisdom-keeper, books I have read, and members of other tribes who are my dear friends. I have studied the Christian religion and ancient teachings of other masters. The ideas \ philosophies in this book and of my art reflect all of these "melting-pot" experiences.

I have made this honest statement about the spiritual philosophies in this book. Whether or not other Indian authors make such a statement; readers should beware that European colonization and forced Christian teachings changed Indian spirituality so long ago that no one really knows what "pure" Indian Spirituality really was (or is).

It is my hope that those who read this book receive spiritual blessings and growth through the experience. It is my hope that I can *spread the good* around a little bit!

Fall 2007, 4th edition: Susan Thomas Underwood is no longer a member of the Loyal Shawnee Tribe, but is now a member of the Cherokee Tribe of N.E. Alabama.

Susan Thomas Underwood

Contents

Introduction

Know *the laws*
and find *the truth.*

Find the truth
and follow *the path.*

Follow the path
and observe *the way.*

You will find you have company.
You will find that Spirit walks with you!

The Laws

Know the Laws. . .

Resurrection

The Universe is energy in constant motion.
There are ebbs and flows;
outcomes and incomes.
And change. . . *always change.*

The physical world reflects this motion
in the cycles of life.
There is Spring and fall, winter and summer,
birth and death; and rebirth. . .
Resurrection!

Einstein proved that even <u>time</u> is relative
in his theory of relativity.
All is relative. . . all is change.
You can count on it.

Be then, as the willow;
learn to bend with the wind!
Always dream, though your dreams may change.
Always produce, though your product may change.
Always love, though your loves may change.
Always live, though your life will change.
You can count on it!

Loss

I become attached to things. I have a special place to put things so that I won't lose them. I am careful when I drive so that I don't damage my car, I take care of my pets so that they won't get lost, have an accident, or get sick and die. Losing things hurts.

I have seen those who are unlucky in love; who are hurt when their lovers walk away. I made sure that when I fell in love that the person was stable, dependable, one who would not do things to hurt me or leave me. I have always shielded myself from loss.

Then, one by one, my beloved pets grow old and die. My cars wear out and I have to replace them. The mate I chose for a lifetime didn't last a lifetime. He died at 42. My heart was destroyed. With all the safeguards I used to avoid a broken heart; it broke anyway. I felt betrayed.

His death was sad to him, too. He hated to leave his family, his horses, his chosen accumulated "things". Custom boots, saddles, bridles and spurs so carefully designed; all things he left behind when he traveled on.

This summer, I lost my mother. She had cancer and her body just gave out. I prayed for her constantly, I practiced spiritual healing on her; the doctors and hospitals did everything they could. But she still died.

There is no way around loss. It is in the great scheme of things; a part of living. I shed my tears and go on. However, knowing that loss is imminent, the joy of each and every moment, each and every loved one, and each and every special "thing", becomes a passion!

The Return

Observing Mon-a-lah, mother earth; I see that Everything we make from her is eventually destroyed. There seems to be an unyielding force that almost immediately begins a process of undoing as soon as we build something. Fences and barns constructed on our ranch begin the return to their mother as soon a we finish building them! Oh, I try to interfere with the process and mend and paint; but as I grow older, the battle seems insurmountable and I am losing my enthusiasm!

I see old cars/equipment fulfill their purpose and begin their return to earth. Works of art, such as the Mona Lisa, yield as museum conservationists attempt to mend her cracks and hold the paint together a little longer Scientists say that even the Titanic, two miles under the ocean, is on the journey home as micro-organisms ingest her mass.

Yes, all things which we create are surely taken away from us; as if mother earth calls them home almost as soon as we take from her. She forgets about none of her off-spring, and does not rest until all are safely home within her bosom.

I look at what we call *living* things and see that they are under the same *law of return*. The decaying tree trunk and leaves on the ground, the decaying body of a two-winged. Yes, even the human body (though we hinder the journey with our elaborate coffins and tombs) all embark on *the return* as soon as creation occurs.

I have heard it said that once the blinding explosion of creation was complete, the force of undoing began. The physical universe seems to reflect this pattern of creation and return. It is my guess that the spirit world reflects this same law.

Souls who separate from the spirit world are immediately drawn back to the Great Good Spirit, Weshemonito's bosom. The journey is a growth experience which cleans the soul in the return. This insures the law of spiritual growth, as everything that happens to us, (whether good or bad in our perception) prepares us for the return to Weshemonito and its perfection. Hence, the moment of separation (whether physical things from Mother Earth, or spiritual souls from Weshemonito), brings about the immediate

Journey of return to the source of origin. This is the
law of return.

To Serve

Most of us know that to serve others is a good
thing. All occupations bring us the opportunity to serve
others: the doctor who serves his patients, the politician
who serves his public, the lawyer who serves justice.
Even a computer programmer or accountant who works
in an office serves others, indirectly, in his/her work!

Those who truly serve and let nothing get in
the way; we know, are on the right path! Unfortunately,
many *serve themselves.* Some doctors take on too many
patients in order to accumulate more money; thus
disserving patients. Politicians fall prey to kick
backs/favors and even one with the best of intentions
can end up serving themselves. Lawyers can get stars in
their eyes and let their egos interfere with the search for
justice. Many people have high ideals, but something
gets in the way and the service to others is lost.

What is the thing that gets in the way? It can be
called greed, selfishness, self-preservation; but the root
of all of these actions is fear. We fear for ourselves, we

fear for our future, we fear we won't be taken care of. We fear we will perish.

There is a promise that when we serve, our needs will be met. The bible says it many ways. In particular. "Commit thy work unto the Lord and then it will succeed". All religions speak of this law, but our fear overpowers our ears. We just can't get it!

As I live my life, I see the law in effect. Those who serve have a glow about them; they are truly happy individuals. Their needs are met, miraculously, in a seemingly effortless way. Spiritual laws begin to work, and all that is needed is provided in order to allow the service to continue. The universe works for us in an equal portion to our work for the universe.

Observing the law and witnessing its results gives one the faith to go out on a limb and into unyielding service. The road to happiness? Find your service and dedicate yourself to it, and all else will fall into place!

Thoughts

A thought seems to be a small thing. We have thoughts that come and go in our lives every day. Some of them are good, some are bad. For the most part, we don't think we have any control over them, feeling somewhat "victims" to them. This is certainly the attitude I used to have about them.

Then, tragedy struck my life. I found myself in an eternal circle of recurring thought. I not only lived through the tragedy, but due to my thoughts, I kept reliving the tragedy. I couldn't get past it. I saw that if I didn't do something, I was going to live this tragedy the rest of my life. I didn't want to be a victim.

I decided that my way out was "thought discipline". So, I devised a plan where I allocated this tragedy a certain amount of "thought" time in a day. After all, I knew that one has to face and work through such events for healthy recovery. Beyond this allocated time, I would give it no more. Every time the event would pop into my mind, I simply pushed it away and refused to indulge. Soon, I began to think of other things; to go on with my life. I became interested in other things; and became involved. For the first time in my life, I saw that I *did* have control over my thoughts!

As I worked through and beyond my tragedy, I began to use this "thought discipline" to improve myself. I had an image of the person I wanted to be, but previously I hadn't an inkling of how to accomplish the reality. I began to *"think" the reality*. Anything that came into my mind that wasn't that reality, I pushed away. It took time, patience, and commitment, but I gradually began to "live" what I "thought". I became the person I wanted to be.

I am an artist. I get an idea for a painting and bounce it around in my mind before I attempt to paint it. I work out the idea: the design, the colors, the perspective, the "image" in my mind before I attempt the reality. I think that every creative person does this: architects, engineers, researchers, inventors, all of them have the "thought" before they create the reality. Is it so difficult to conceive that we "become" our thoughts; that negative thoughts begat negative behavior, and positive thoughts begat positive behavior? Maybe thoughts are NOT small things; maybe they are very powerful.

This is something to consider the next time we look at another and think negative things about them, or look in the mirror and put ourselves down and feel ourselves worthless. Or, when we look at our nation or the world and see only negative things. We can not control others, only ourselves; and a lot can be done within our minds to make our little corner of the world a good place. It all begins with our thoughts.

The Mirror

It is not only the Native Way that teaches the spiritual *law of Mirroring*. I am by no means an expert on world religions, but I have heard several New Age teachings discuss this law, and Jesus Christ taught this concept often in such statements as, "an eye for an eye" and "If a man taketh thy shirt, give to him also thy cloak", and, "turn the other cheek".

In the journey to become our highest possible selves, this is a law that one must confront. It is, quite simply, getting back what you give. As one looks into a mirror, the mirror reflects back what he projects, as others reflect back to us that which we project to them.

This simple concept can affect our lives dearly! I see it in action every moment of my day. I have a store where I deal with the public daily. If a customer comes in with a bad attitude it is my first response to be rude back to him. However, I am aware of this law, catch myself, and project love and goodness back to him. Now, he leaves my store with a possibility of absorbing that goodness and love and projecting it onto someone else. I have improved the world a little bit. Sometimes, these "bad attitudes" come in daily and, little by little, change into pleasant customers. This law is not only effective in working with two-leggeds, but also the four-leggeds.

Awareness of this law can improve our lives. I've had bosses, co-workers, and students that I despised. Of course, as I projected despise to them, they projected those feelings back to me. As I grew into a more spiritual person and aware of the "mirroring" that was going on, I knew I had to change my thinking towards them. I rationalized that each person is a result of his/her own experience; and there is a justified reason for the qualities about that person that I despise. Who knows what happened in their childhood that may have made them selfish, critical, unbending, or. . . whatever? This helped me to understand them better, even allowed me to gain sympathy for them and project love towards them. Before long I projected a different attitude and my relationship with them improved as they "mirrored" back my feelings.

It saddens me to observe Native Americans, and many African Americans, who wear a chip on their shoulders because of past (and present) oppression of their people by European pioneers of today's America. Who can say it isn't justified? I view what happened to my Shawnee ancestors who fought for Ohio until there was hardly any tribe left; to be a holocaust equal to the Jewish holocaust of Germany. No, ethnic cleansing is not right, never has been and never will be; nor is slavery! But in order to improve the lives of ourselves and our descendants, we simply must get over it and move on with our lives. The "chip" is passed from parents to children from generation to generation. And with each generation, the "chip" diminishes the quality of life, continuing oppression through the law of mirroring.

The key to mastering the law of mirroring is to work on a mental/causal level rather than an emotional/reactionary level. In other words, think before you react. This will always put you in command!

Limitations

Counselors fight negative "programming" within their clients in order to get them past hangups which hold them back. As a public school art teacher, many children came into my class and the first thing out of their mouths was, "I can't draw". I got so sick of the phrase, "I can't", that I outlawed it in my class. We all hear phrases such as, "I can't do math", or "I am not athletic"; in fact, many times we hear them come out of our own mouths! Often, if these thoughts were traced back, we will learn *we picked them up from our parents.*

And so, we see that our own thoughts can not only limit us, but also the *thoughts of others.* In our quest to become the best that we can be, we must learn not to take on the negative thoughts that others project on to us. It is easy to understand how a child can have low self esteem when a parent calls them "stupid". But, even as adults, we can find ourselves taking on such labels.

When I was a schoolteacher, I occasionally had problems with parents who would criticize my teaching. On one such occasion, I was discussing with my counselor friend a complaint which had been turned in to the Dept. of Human Services and had prompted an investigation. I complained, "They say I am abusing their children!". My counselor friend looked at me and said, "Well, are you what they say you are? Are you abusing their children?" "No", I snapped back, "I am a very good art teacher and I am in no way abusing their children!" "Then, that settles it. You know who you are, that you are not a monster and that you are a good art teacher. Hold onto that, and your belief in yourself will get you through this." And, it did.

13

I now share this experience with others who take on what others say about them. As a friend confided to me that most people in her community thought she was crazy, I asked her how she saw herself. She responded that she had grown beyond society's boundaries of looking, acting, and living a certain way. She dresses the way she wants, and lives in a way that she feels is pleasing to her Creator; being kind to all: two legged, winged, and four legged. I told her that she must hold onto that and not let others tell her who or what she is. It is of no matter, I told her, but her image of herself was what I saw in her also.

All of this goes back to the law of mirroring and "taking on" what others project on to you. It probably reflects their own low self-worth; having to run down others in order to feel better about themselves. When we understand this concept, it becomes easy to disclaim such potentially damaging statements and rise to a level of *laughing it off*. Thus, we are able to use the law of mirroring in *our* favor, and project to others our wonderful, true, unique selves.

Longevity

Listen to those who say they know; eat only certain foods and do all the things they say to do. Stay away from all the things they say are bad, and take all your medicines. Go and visit your doctor, give him your money, and be sure to live close to a good hospital.

Do all these things and, whether you are sleeping in your bed, visiting that hospital, or dancing a jig. . . not one moment before nor one moment after. . . *you will die at your appointed time.*

Eye Of The Tornado

I have traveled many miles and visited with many people and I find that each of them has personal problems. We all envision, *that person over there* as having an ideal life; but when you talk to them, it is quite another story. The poor complain of lack, the rich complain of hustlers. The beautiful complain of "fake" friends, and the non-beautiful complain of prejudice. There are those who lose their parents at an early age and are raised in foster homes or orphanages. There are those whose parents abuse them and scar them

15

physically and emotionally for life. There is no, "beautiful life" in reality!

That is as it should be, for we do not come to Earth from the spirit world for rewards. We all come with an agenda. Struggles make us grow; they force us to climb higher on the spiritual ladder. This is the purpose of our earth walk.

As we endure, some of us envision the easy way out; ending it all. Some even take this option. Indian teachings do not consider this the eternal unforgivable sin; but does frown on suicide. It is an ungrateful act towards Creator and the breaking of a life contract. The contract must be fulfilled before one can go beyond it; therefore one's next life must parallel the conditions of the last one. In other words, one must simply start all over in the next life and do it all over again!

Indian teachings tell us that when we find ourselves in the middle, or *eye of the tornado*, the only escape is *UP.* This is a time to take the focus off the four directions and look to the fifth direction. That is where we see and focus on Creator and It's Divine Will. And, what is Divine Will? A continuing thread within all world religions and those who have crossed over to the other side and come back to tell about it, is LOVE.

It is understandably difficult to turn one's head up while our lives are in total chaos! It is natural to focus on the chaos and say to ourselves, "poor me, look at this and look at that". . . and on and on. Being down and depressed is a very selfish thing! "**I** am broke, **I** am fat and ugly, nobody likes **Me**." Such selfish motives may be why we are in a bind anyway!

We must forget about ourselves and look to others. One can independently become a Good Samaritan, or volunteer at churches and charities of his/her choice. The key is focus on *Creator* and spreading *It's* love around. Before long, the chaos has worked itself out and the healing has begun. This is the *law of the fifth direction.*

The Master

The master remains constant despite any changes around him. He walks his path with a relaxed confidence, for he knows that Creator has assigned a task and there is not one thing he can do against it; even if he so desired. He knows the *Law of Divine Will.*

He never finds fault nor distributes punishment, for he trusts justice to the perfection of The Great Mystery. He is governed entirely by the *law of love.*

The *law of soul growth*; promises that when one needs a master, one will appear. Only a few will recognize him as such; for he will more likely be a servant than a man of the world.

Open thine eyes and see thy master; for there is no light which casts no shadow!

The Truth

*Know the laws
and find the truth. . .*

The Truth

We cannot find the truth
it finds us.
We must learn to recognize it.

I have learned that truth changes.
When I was a young girl,
I found the truth.
Now, in my middle age,
I know a different truth!
I expect when I am old,
I will know a different truth
from the one I know now.

I probably knew a different truth
before I came to this earth,
and will know a different one in
my life beyond this one.

I think truth has a name,
it is called *Growth*.

Teachers

Teachers come in many forms. In fact, those in my life who have been called "teacher" sometimes taught me the least; maybe just what a teacher is not.

One time, a spider taught me a lesson. I was allowing her to live in my bedroom window to catch flies. But one night, she bit me. I learned not to lay down with a spider. She has a place, and I a place, but our places are not together. Well, spiders have many forms, and now; I live by this lesson.

I have a wolf who has taught me many lessons. He has a very large, warm heart, and loves me with all of it! He has a mind of his own. He knows what I don't allow him to do; but he sneaks and does it anyway. This helps me understand my husband and my children. They love me with all their hearts; but they are separate from me and have their own minds. They may do some things I don't approve of; but that doesn't mean they don't love me. I live by this lesson now.

I have a relative who is very angry. She yells at her husband and children and says horrible things to them and to others who get in her way. Throughout my life as I observed her, I swore I would never yell at my children like that, or treat my husband with such contempt. She taught me as much about what a good wife and mother are as those I had known who were good examples. She taught me what a good wife and mother is NOT.

A good student must be a careful observer with a discerning eye. A good student must know who his teachers really are.

<u>Meeting Others</u>

I think that I am a special person. I have great talents; things I alone do better than anyone else I know. I know that I am smart and, as I grow older; I grow wise. I know that I am very sensitive, and have deep feelings about things.

I have great hurts that I am recovering from. I have suffered great personal losses and still, I continue on. These things I know.

One day, I realized of all the masses of people; millions of them, billions of them, that each of them feels special, too. Then, I looked into my wolf's eyes, and I could see that he too, feels special. His eyes said he has suffered hurt and loss, and yet continues on. . . just like me. And, I looked into my horse's eyes, and the eyes of Eagle and Owl; and they all told me this is true for them.

This great truth came to me: The meeting of one to another, whether two legged or four, two winged or finned; is the *meeting of two souls.*

About Religion

Once, I was a church Indian. They told me, "God is perfect, and to get into His perfect world (heaven), I must believe in Jesus.". I liked the things this Jesus said, and so, I accepted their church.

I went to their church and listened to their words. There, they said that God is jealous, and that he likes gold and silver and the temples they build for Him with it. Their God likes money, and wants ours! They said He hates some people, and sometimes instructs them to kill those He hates. They said He judges and punishes us!

This did not sound like a perfect God to me, and is not like this Jesus they told me about. I think these white men are confused. I believe Creator sent Jesus to these white ones to *try* and set them straight!

And so, I turned to the Great Good Spirit; my Creator who loves me. Who loves all the same, as It is Father to all. Gold and silver are Its children, not Its possessions. And, It has no interest in the paper called money. Indian's Creator knows nothing about hate, jealousy, murder, or materialism. It is as separate from these things as there is space to separate. We know that It is good, and that is why we call It, "The Great Good Spirit- Weshemonito", and we do not fear It. There is much we do not know about It. That is why It is called, "The Great Mystery".

Forgiveness

I have found
there are many blessings
on the other side
of forgiveness.

Just as I have found
there are many blessings
on the other side
of, "I'm sorry".

Wisdom

We are taught the elderly have wisdom. I have found something to be true about wisdom... it does not necessarily come with age!

I have an aunt who is now in her nineties. She has always been beautiful; spending hours in the bathroom in front of the mirrors. There are mirrors all over her house, several in every room. She loves to look at herself. She has always adored beauty, choosing her beautiful relatives as her favorites! I like beauty, too, and seek out beautiful things to look at. Beautiful things make me feel good. Yes, beautiful is good.

I see beauty in many things. I see beauty in a small child playing in a mud puddle, and a mother who allows a child this kind of freedom. I see beauty in an old horse with a broken body, who has served his owners well. I see beauty in my husband who has gray hair, aging skin, and bulges in different places than in his younger days! He is beautiful to me because of the loyalty he has shown me, because of the love and support he has given me through the years. My old cat is beautiful to me.

I am growing older too, and am overweight and too busy to concern myself with beauty. Several years ago, I saw my aunt. After many years apart, rather than give me a hug; she hung her head and asked me how I could let myself go the way I had! Every time I have seen her since, she does the same thing. I am no longer one of her favorites! I had not realized that she liked me because I was beautiful.

How many times are we astounded by a wise statement from a young child? Not often, but it happens. And sometimes, we are astounded by the ignorance of an elder. Lessons are gifts as we walk this road called life, and wisdom is our reward. However, it is possible to complete the journey and entirely miss the boat!

Miracles

Miracles can be a daily occurrence in our lives, we must first be open to them and observant. If we do not believe they can happen, we do not look for them; and therefore, do not see them.

A miracle can be small or large, and the small miracle is just as marvelous as the great one. Spirit is not dazzled by size, quantity, or other qualitative values we two-leggeds put on things. What can be called a

miracle? Each individual must judge for
himself/herself; we all know when one happens to us.

For example, one day when I taught school, I
was drawing a picture of particular importance to me. I
changed buildings during the day, and when I put up my
supplies, I found that the photo I was working from was
gone. To my horror, I wondered how I could retrace
my steps and find the photo. It was terribly windy
Oklahoma day and now, school was out and children
were boarding the buses and loading in their parents
cars. It would be impossible to find that photo in all
that confusion. I dismissed the hope of it's recovery.

Leaving in my car, something told me to turn
left instead of right, and as I passed the parking lot, (not
knowing why), I parked in an empty space. I got out of
my car, took two steps, and there on the ground, in the
wind and mass confusion, was my photo! Just for me,
it lie there; waiting.

A miracle? I thought so. Today I have a
wonderful painting of me and my daughter, embraced
in love during a very difficult time in our lives, because
Spirit provided a tiny little miracle!

On a larger scale, I was traveling to an art show
in Florida, zooming down the freeway. I glanced at a
semi truck ahead of me and a vision flashed before me
of that truck spinning out of control, crossing five lanes

of traffic and crashing in the center medium. I looked at the truck again (it was traveling safely down the highway), and wondered why that vision came to me. At that instant, I noticed every vehicle ahead of me had brake lights flashing, and slammed on my brakes just in time to avoid a collision. As we crept along at 15 mph, I thought, "This is why I saw the vision, there is probably a semi truck crashed ahead of me in the center median". A few minutes later, I passed the semi truck cab, upside down with its trailer and cargo of pipe spread everywhere! The vision had been a warning, and I was astonished and very thankful. The warning could have saved my life, and I consider it a large miracle.

As I look back on my life, I can see many miracles; miracles that have shaped my life and lead me to the place where I am today. My life is very full and interesting, and I look for and *see* miracles every day!

The Path

*Find the Truth
and follow The Path. . .*

<u>Doors</u>

I used to think that any door could be opened. Some stood freely open, some could be opened easily; some were harder to penetrate. Sometimes you had to knock, sometimes bang, sometimes charge; but always, a door could be opened.

Goals in my life were accomplished in this way. No matter what I wanted; I accomplished it because I was willing to pound and pound and pound against its door.

But I no longer live this philosophy, because I walk *the path* Creator prepares for me. Maybe I am not supposed to pass through a particular door. I have quit deciding which doors I wish to pass through. I have learned to let Creator open them for me.

You see, I am a rancher and I raise cattle. I know that my cattle and I do not speak the same language, and I cannot tell them where I want them to go. The way I show them is by opening gates. If I don't want them to go into this or that pasture; I shut the gate. If I want them in a certain place, I open a gate. If there is no gate, I get between them and the place I do not want them to be with my horse or my truck, I provide obstacles. I guide them in this way.

Because the language of this world and the spirit world is different; communication is obscure. I have learned that Creator guides me in the way that I guide my cattle. Now, I look for open doors, for they are open for a reason. Doors that are shut, are shut for a reason. I am not saying the path is easy; there is much work walking the path Creator places before us. However, our precious energy does not have to be spent pounding against doors. Our energy can be saved for the path beyond the door. I'm saying to look for the open doors; for they mark your special path, your purpose, your dreams.

Security

I observe those who provide themselves security through various means. Some go to college to become doctors or lawyers in order to become the most highly paid professionals. Others may marry a highly paid professional to secure a lifetime of good income. There are those who come to a wealthy person at the end of life in order to acquire wealth upon the death of that person.

There seems to be no thought of the price of security gained in this way. Yes, security is gained, but is there a price? What about the spiritual price of practicing a profession for monetary rewards, and not following one's calling? What about marrying a person for their income and not out of love? What about the karmatic debt of taking the life wealth of another in order to secure one's own future?

The money may pile up, but is it ever enough? The college degrees may pile up, but are there ever enough? When I was very young, I desired college degrees and earned them, and I desired a pile of money; all in an attempt to become secure.

Then one day Creator said to me, "Set aside your degrees and the job they brought you and walk this path I have chosen for you.". It was *a path on the edge* of a cliff! Now I do this work that Creator has asked me to do. Somehow I have all that I need and I am happier now than I was before. Somehow, I am secure.

Fear

I know people who say that this world is much more evil now than it was in the past. We hear reports each day through the media of thefts, murders, rapes, incest; and the list goes on. I have relatives who set by their television and hang on to every word of these reports. They center their lives around them, and have many rules to follow. They don't go out before or after certain hours, they lock all their doors at all times, they watch their children like captives. When I go and visit them, I can't keep all their safety rules straight, and am always being scolded for being careless, ignorant.

I believe the world is as it has always been. I know there was evil in medieval days; monarchs who kept their people in poverty and inflicted cruel punishments over insignificant infractions. Dungeons, beheadings, torture; we see in history such horrible inhumanities! I look at more recent times of the Jewish and the Native American Holocaust, Stalin's Russia, the Wild West; the list goes on. Yes, there is, was, and will always be that dark side of humanity.

I do not live a careless life, nor an ignorant one. But, I do feel I have a destiny. I feel I will meet death when and how it is written in the book of life. I came to Earth with a large agenda. I have many things to do, and I must make each moment count! I cannot spend my time looking out the window of a locked house.

The path I have come to walk is not an easy or safe one. I must travel the highways and circulate among people. I have to go out late at night, spend nights on the road, and meet strangers on a daily basis. I have a store that could attract thieves.

Creator gives to us the opportunities, physical means, strengths, skills, and courage to walk our paths of destiny. My path may be more dangerous than

another's. I do what I have to do; but I am aware. I pay
attention, I listen, I make judgments each day. I let
Creator guide me.

Whatever we focus on becomes our reality;
whether it is goodness, happiness, success, or evil,
anger, and fear. A little fear can make us careful, but
too much fear can stifle us. It can keep us form doing
what we came here to do!

Integrity

Integrity can mean something different to
everyone, but my dictionary calls it "rightness". This is
something that everyone wants to possess. As we look
around us, and within us, we see that some have it and
others do not. I even see it, or a lack of it, in the four
leggeds!

When I think about what keeps us from having
it, I think of fear. Why does one do dishonorable acts in
order to have wealth, or the *things* that show wealth? It
is probably due to a fear of not being accepted by one's
peers-or fear of alienation/rejection. We can trace most
of our acts of "wrongness" back to a fear of some sort:
lack of love, security, acceptance, or just lack.

When we confront our fears, this is the first step to gaining integrity. "Why do I lie, steal, put others down, compromise my values, etc.?", and what caused the underlying fear for these actions? Maybe it was a childhood event, or an adult loss through divorce or death. Confronting the event can help us get rid of the resulting fear, and thus the wrongful actions it causes, enabling us to gain integrity, or "rightness".

When we face our fears, that is when the Great Good Spirit can really use us to further It's divine plan. The work that I currently do is Native American inspirational art, writing and public speaking. I didn't come upon this of my own intent! In fact, my husband often reminds me that, had I not confronted my fears and always taken the higher path, I may now be a public school librarian! You see, I began my career as an art teacher. The school administration said they had to lay me off as an art teacher, but that I could have a job as a librarian if I was willing to go back to college and get accredited. My need for security made me consider their offer, as the area where I live is very rural and a good job, let alone an art job, is *very* difficult to find. But, knowing that I was *not* put on this earth to be a librarian, I declined the position and accepted the lay off. I rationalized that I had been poor in my early married years and was nonetheless very happy. Actually the struggle (in hindsight) was fun and exciting. If worse came to worse, I knew I could be poor again and still be happy. But, do you know that I am not poor and

Creator used all those events to put me where It wanted me. Likewise, I try to maintain a certain level of detachment for my current work, as I may again be moved into another area of service.

When we rise above fear, we open the door to "rightness". Think about the war hero who overcomes a fear of death to save lives! Think about the person who overcomes fear of lack and returns a lost wallet full of cash! When I think of heroes, I think of our great Shawnee chief, Tecumseh, or Martin Luther King, or Jesus Christ. I think about their lives, and the fears they had to overcome in order to do what they did. And, it strengthens my personal quest for integrity.

The Approach

In my work as a Native American artist who's work is of a spiritual nature, I have opportunities to discuss spirituality with many people. I am constantly intrigued in the diversity of humanity's concept of the Great Good Spirit, Weshemonito.

Our Native American concept of This Spirit is certainly one of a different twist. Although we speak to

Weshemonito on occasion, much of our focus of worship is spent *listening*. How do we listen? Many of our ceremonies center on listening: such as the sweat lodge and the vision quest. These ceremonies include hours of personal sacrifice, cleansing, and *silence* in order to invite Weshemonito's communication. A religion which centers on prayer is missing at least half of what worship should be, as prayer-communication to Creator-must be offset with meditation-Creator's communication back to us. How would you like to have an encounter with a person who completely dominated the conversation, never letting up so that you could speak back? How frustrated Weshemonito must become with one who only speaks to It!

While many religions seem to use Creator as a means to get things, the Native focus is completely different. Our focus is in *thanking* It! Many of our dances have to do with thanking Creator for the good life that we have. Our ceremonies and prayer are centered around thanks also. While our worship time centers on thanks, we do not spend a lot of time in asking for things. Even our way of asking is different; we just thank ahead of time! "Thank you so much, Weshemonito, for the health of our people, and for this good harvest we are about to receive!", this is a typical Indian prayer.

I like to do things for others, but if I receive no thanks, I loose much of my motivation. Would you do and do and do for a person who never offers thanks in return? No, I would think not. Shouldn't Weshemonito feel this way also? Who among us has nothing to thank Weshemonito for? Even in our worst of times, do we have shelter, do we have air to breathe, food to eat, family to lean on? When I lost my husband, and then later my mother, I could still look around and see a father, a sister, a son, and a daughter. Not to mention my four legged loved ones!

No matter what religion one subscribes to, it is important to think for oneself and not let that religion dictate thought and action. Of course, it is very easy to just sit and be told how to worship; but to think out for one's self the appropriate way to approach the Great Good Spirit may take some effort. In fact, I put a lot of effort into it. However, when I really think about how important this act is, *actually approaching Creator,* I tremble at It's power and know I cannot put enough effort into my approach.

The Way

*Follow the Path
and observe the Way. . .*

The Way

It is not only important to walk down *the path* that Creator has set before us; but we must walk it in *the way.*

The way is all the little things one does along the path. What kind of product is being produced? Is there a large pile of money? Is there a large pile of accumulated physical things, such as cars, houses, property? Are there many degrees and awards on the wall?

All of these things can be used in a positive way. Possibly, when one accumulates them as a means to a positive end, they can certainly be good. However, if one accumulates them as an end; this may not be so good!

Our physical body is just a wrapping around soul; as possibly Mon-a-lah (Mother Earth) and Her creatures may be a wrapping around The Great Good Spirit. Without the wrapping, we are all the same inside: *soul.* The product of soul is manifested in the wrapping and the things that it produces. Therefore, the product gives us an insight into the soul.

A pile of money can be used to help the poor: not only to feed and shelter them, but also to create businesses which provide jobs, services, etc. Degrees can place us in professions where we can help others: such as teachers, business executives, healers, lawyers, etc. Again, the *product* is the focus, not the degree. An award is a "thank you" from those whom one has helped or served, and is the result of a good product. The award should not be the focus.

Even though the physical universe is a manifestation of The Great Good Spirit's thoughts, upon leaving the physical universe and crossing over into the spirit world, one stands naked. All that matters at that time are the spirit *things* (product) that we have accumulated, such as:

How many souls were *helped* because you smiled at them when they were having a bad day?
How many souls did you *lift up* with your words when they were feeling down and depressed?
How many souls did you *love and show love to*, even though they were embodied in physical shells of oppressed races?
How many times did you lay open your own wounds, so that you could *comfort* another soul?
How much *good* did you spread around when you walked the earth?

In other words, how many souls did you *serve?* (Encompassed in this word *soul* is also those of the four-leggeds, two-winged, and finned.)

On the other hand, one can also apply these same words in the negative, such as: How many souls did you *hurt, oppress, hate?* Is this the product with which you will cross over? I am afraid I will have some of that, too. But, I am doing my best keep the negative to a minimum!

Think about these things as you travel the path, for *the way* is the product that we spread along the path!

Our Mother

Creator designed Earth as our mother. She gives us water, food, shelter, and fuel to warm the cold nights. She provides these things to all living things and not to just the two-leggeds, and we all know these things.

But, did you know that Mother Earth, Mon-a-lah, will soothe you when you are down, and energize you when you are depleted?

The next time you feel depressed, do not go to the White Man's house or city. Go to your Earth Mother. Seek out a quiet place where Mother Earth is natural and undisturbed by White Man. Lay down upon

42

Her; let Her sun cradle and warm your body. Let Her gentle breeze caress your face, and let Her waters restore your life. Listen to Her music, it will melt your troubles away. You will walk away a new person.

But remember; return to her as you would your own mother. Be good to her and give Her gifts occasionally. Our Mother needs our love just as we need hers. It is all in the balance.

Blessings

Many of us are suspicious of things that come our way. Basically, we rely on the appearance of things to judge whether they are good or bad for us. We think we know what blessings look like.

In my life I have found that some nice packages turned out to be bad for me. I think we have all had this experience. We can learn this lesson from Mother Earth; for some of her prettiest packages are the most deadly: i.e., poisonous plants, snakes, insects, etc., are the most beautiful species on earth.

On the other hand, some packages will surprise you! Do not be quick to judge! Some time after my first husband died, I decided to get out and date and a wonderful man came into my life. I was simply wanting a nice person to date; I had no interest in a serious relationship. After all, I had had the love of my life and we all know that there is only one of those. There would be no one else for me and I was resigned to it! However, as I continued to see this man, it seemed he was perfect for me. I spoke with Creator about it, and Creator said, "Yes, I have sent him to you.". "But," I told Creator, "it is not yet time for another mate for me. My parents are not ready for another son nor my children another father. Nor is my sister ready for another brother or my relatives another cousin! This can not be, another mate for me. . . already?"

Creator said to me, "This is the man I have chosen for you and this is the right time. Now, take him or leave him!"! I now have a new husband.

Another time I was attending an art show and circumstances lead me to a couple who owned a wolf. They told me their sad story: "We raised our wolf in our home; and as he grew larger, he destroyed everything there. Then, we moved him outside and chained him. The children of our town will not leave him alone. They either want to play with him or annoy him. We cannot afford a tall fence. He is biting at the children now, and we know it is a matter of time before someone is hurt and the city will ask us to put him down. You have a ranch, and we want our wolf to run free. Please take our wolf!" I told them I would think about it.

I went directly to Creator about this! I said, "Although I love all animals, I have never felt a strong connection to dog. Am I to begin my connection to dog by putting a full grown wolf in the cab of my truck and traveling on a three hour trip home with him? What if he doesn't like me? What if he goes for my throat while I am driving?" Creator said, "Allow wolf to come, he is a gift."

I replied, "But, I am a rancher, I raise cattle. What business do I have with a *wolf* on a ranch? What will my husband say. What will my son, who manages the ranch, say?" Creator said, "Wolf is your gift, he has medicine for you. He is my blessing to you, take him!"

"But", I said, "I am a very busy person. I am doing your work, walking the path you made just for me! I do not have the time to commit to adapting this animal to a new home. He will need much attention; attention I just don't have time to give! Surely, I would be crazy to take this wolf home with me!" Creator said, "He is your gift, take him or leave him. It is your choice!" Now, I have a wonderful wolf in my life.

I've had a flat tire which led me back into my house just in time to receive a call from an old friend. I have lost jobs which allowed me to receive better opportunities. I see packages throughout each day that I turn away, only to wonder later, " What blessing may I have rejected?". For instance, one morning a man came into my store and bought a bag of ice. He commented he had just come from a store where he had purchased ice, but forgot it! A thought flashed into my mind, "Make this bag of ice this man's gift, it would make his day!". But, I rationalized that our store needed all the money it could get, and I charged the man $.59 for the ice, apologizing for his misfortune. Moments later, I realized I had missed a blessing. For $.59 I could have made a difference in this man's day, and made myself feel very good in the process. . . a missed blessing.

I try to live my life with no regrets, and so accordingly, I pay attention to all the packages!

Oneness

Interacting with people of all nations, I am often confronted with the statement, "Indians worship nature". It is difficult to come back to such a statement, for obviously its maker has limited concept of Indian spirituality. For the most part, I would say the statement is untrue. On the other hand, we believe the earth is a manifestation of the Great Good Spirit, Weshemonito; thus all things come from it. We hold in reverence all things created by it, and one could accurately say those things are also of it, and thus, it. So maybe, in a round about way, the statement is, at least not far from the truth.

All things being of Weshemonito manifests a oneness through which Its spirit flows. Thus, all things possess this spirit , a binding force that connects us all. The Indians say, "All my relations". We are related to the earth, the trees, the four-leggeds; we are all related!

Being related to all things opens us to inter-communication. Did you know you can communicate with all things? Have you listened to the wind? Have you listened to the trees, the hawk, the coyote? Did you know you can communicate back? Not only verbally (which I enjoy doing at my country place), but through *telepathy!* Look at the cardinal and tell him he is beautiful, touch the tree and tell him /her you appreciate Its service, tell the animal who provided your meal that you appreciate Its sacrifice. Revere all things, this is the Red way.

The Others

There seems to be a race in our world today. We don't even know what the race is all about, or where it leads us. We just race.

Many two-leggeds encourage their children to move to the big city and earn a lot of money. This place is "where it's at" for the jobs and the *things* that our society values these days. Most two leggeds there get caught up in *the race* where the life of Mon-a-lah, our Mother Earth, and her *other* creatures become a hazy memory of the past.

Unfortunately, such childhood memories of our older two-leggeds may not be possible for their children. Growing up in the city seems, unless there is a conscious effort on the part of parents to teach the wonderfulness of the four-leggeds and two-winged, to instill values of twisted social pressures such as wealth and materialism. Young children who have not yet been affected by these pressures naturally gravitate towards animals. I have witnessed pleads by young children to own a dog, or other four-leggeds; only to be told by the parent that these animals were, "too much trouble", or, "dirty and nasty". As time goes by, these children gradually abandon their pleads and go to the mall and enjoy shopping (or shop-lifting) and playing video games, etc. Separation from the natural world is eventually accepted.

I have heard that the world population is expected to double within the next 20 years. The future for the four-legged and two-winged does not look promising. There are a few two-leggeds today who still value *the others* and have set aside wildlife reserves for them. However, what will happen as mass population explosion encroaches? I see the fate of the four-leggeds and two-winged to be the same as the American Indian. We were told to move, and so we did. Then as our old lands became settled and the white appetite for land grew, we were asked to move again, and again and again. Lastly, we were moved to Indian Territory and told these would always be our lands as long as the grass grows and the river flows. But, I guess in 70 years the grass ceased to grow and the rivers ceased to flow; because they took Indian Territory away from us and made the new state, Oklahoma!

One can argue that domesticated four-leggeds serve us; give us companionship and food. Is there really any reason for *the wild ones?* The American Indian and those who live close to *the wild ones* know. We know that Creator uses them in It's communication to us. We know to watch them for the signs that they bring, and we hold them in great respect and reverence.

When my first husband was battling cancer; a *sparrow* seemed to follow him around. As he sat at the kitchen table crying just after diagnosis, a little sparrow sat close to him on the window sill. *Wiskilootha* did not fly away, but lingered there, giving him a message of Divine love and a promise that the Great Good Spirit was *aware*. Another time I took him in a wheelchair to the hospital garden, and a sparrow sat in the bush beside us. As my husband approached his last moments on earth, a sparrow flew into the window beside him; hitting itself hard against the glass and falling to the ground. Another sparrow did the same thing. In addition, one of our *cows* got into our yard and peered into the window at him; a strange event that happened neither before nor after his death.

As my husband walked the valley of death, *owl* moved into our yard. As time ran out for him, *Myaathwe* began to hoot during the day (normally owl only hoots at dusk or night). As they removed my husband's body from our home, owl set perched on our roof and hooted the death chant. Owl remained with us through the funeral, and then mysteriously went away.

And, that is not all! Six years later, my mother was diagnosed with cancer. I tried to be optimistic as she fought a difficult battle. About a month earlier, owl had come to me at night and set in the tree beside my bedroom window. He hooted and hooted until I awakened. I heard him as I lay there becoming awake. Finally, I got up and went to the window. He repeated his message to me, and I told him, "I understand.". He then flew away. The day she died, I was at an art show back East. The morning of her death I was awakened by a *crow* cawing five times, then a break; five times, then a break. This sequence was repeated over and over. I went to a phone and called home, and found out she had *crossed over*. I told my husband, who is from the East, of this event, and he said that there are not any owls back East anymore. Maybe Creator sent *Hataakwa* (crow) instead?

As my mother died of cancer, my husband's father was diagnosed! His fight lasted eight months; and can you guess what happened? One night as my husband smoked a cigarette at the fire place, the owl hooted to him down the chimney! The next night, the same thing happened. I told him his father would die with a month. And, he did.

Owl visited me one other time, and it was during my father-in-law's battle with cancer. It happened as it had with my mother; owl awakened me at night beside my window. I thought about who could be dying, and told my husband his father's time may be close. But, within the month no human had died. I thought back as I wondered who the owl was preparing us to loose. I remembered my mother's cat had died. This very old cat had been her faithful companion for nearly 20 years; she literally mourned herself to death after mother's passing. This sad event would also lead one to the realization that our four legged cousins may be equally as important to Creator as ourselves.

Such events are told among Indians freely; but we hesitate to share them with our white cousins, who don't seem to value the lives or worth of *the others*. An Indian friend shared her story: upon her father's death a bald eagle flew over his grave as they buried him. A chilling event she will always remember! Such events happen not only concerning death, but also about the concerns of life. Most humans have lost the connection to the natural world and can no longer recognize the signs even if *the others* are there to send them out. Our Native American teaching connects each animal to an energy and the medicine it holds for us two leggeds. This is true not only of the animals, but also the plants and minerals. Native American teaching centers on Mon-a-lah and all Her inhabitants, not just Man.

The answer to this urban trend: I know not! One cannot control global events, but we do have a finite effect on our own lives. At this time in our world, no matter where one lives, nature is still relatively close at hand. We can all do our part in preserving Mon-a-lah and her creatures; and we *must* teach our children these things. We must realize that the future of Kokomthena (Mon-a-lah personal Shawnee name, i.e. Mon-a-lah Kokomthena) and Her inhabitants, while we tend to empower ourselves with this fate, is ultimately intertwined within the *grand Divine plan!*

Beauty

When I was young, I worked at being beautiful. I thought that was all I had to offer the world. I kept my body slender, I finished my nails, my hair, and painted my face. Inside of me, on the other hand, was lacking. I felt empty and depressed. I felt I had little worth. These were some of my most unhappy days; when I was beautiful.

Now I am older and would not be considered beautiful anymore. Outside, I am lacking. Oh, I am clean and groomed, but I no longer spend my time painting my face or tending my nails and hair, and my body is out of shape! Today, I tend my soul.

I groom my thoughts, culling out all the negative ones-even about myself-that may creep in. I spend time with Creator and talk to It, and listen back. I concern myself with doing what It asks me to do; accomplishing great, good things. I work at being kind to others, two legged and four; making their day better because our paths crossed. My focus has changed from the outside things, to the inside things. But, I am no longer beautiful.

The Destination

The passions of this world: lust, anger, greed, attachment, and vanity are the toys of Matshemonito, the mischievous spirit who distracts us from the good. Such passions hold us down on an earthly plane, disabling us from looking to the heavens and concentrating on spiritual growth.

Before we can look up, we must stop looking down! Oh, we may not master these passions; but as a river surely flows to the ocean, these elements may alter our course but we can ultimately reach our destination: that great ocean of love from whence we came, that place where Creator IS.

Therefore first: solve the mysteries of thy little self before ye can seek the great mystery of Divine. . . and become thy highest possible self!

Walking With Spirit

As I grow older, I become more aware of the Great Good Spirit, "Weshemonito". At first, I did everything I could to get close to this Spirit: I prayed, I worshiped, I studied. I knocked and knocked at It's door. But always, I remained here and Spirit was over there.

Then, I got quiet. Because of a great personal tragedy; I couldn't pray, or worship, or study anymore. I only sat in quiet. Then, I began to hear; and *I listened.*

One day, I turned around and I was there where Spirit IS. Or, maybe Spirit was where I was. Now, there are still times when I am too overwhelmed to pray, and I cannot worship, nor do I have time to study. I am too busy walking with Spirit.

About the Author
Susan Thomas Underwood

Susan grew up in Northeastern Oklahoma on her family ranch near Lenapah which she now operates with her son. She is a member of the Cherokee Tribe of N.E. Alabama. She lives a life close to nature, is active in her tribe, and lives the traditional Indian ways.

Susan was married to her high school sweetheart, Joe Thomas, for 22 years when he developed kidney cancer and *crossed over* in 1991. At this time, Susan taught art in public school and produced wildlife art. After his death, her art suddenly included Native Americans. She completed 15 "grief" paintings and curated Joe's memorial exhibit which toured 4 cities in 1992-93. In 1994, Susan took the name of her new husband, Donald Underwood, and created Underwood Studio; devoting full-time to producing her Native American heart-felt art and traveling the Indian Art show circuit.

Susan's art depicts Native American Spiritual philosophies, some original to her own thinking. A poem or explanation for each painting has become an intricate part of the art, and this practice opened the door to the writings within this book.

Works of
Susan Thomas Underwood

This book and other products by the artist are available through her studio at:

Underwood Studio
Route 1, Box 188a
Delaware, OK. 74027
(918) 467-3378
website: **truthart.net**

PRODUCTS AVAILABLE

SEEKS THE TRUTH, A Philosophical Search For Truth Through Native American Teachings, published in 2000 by O-SI-YO Truthart Publisher, $10.99

ANIMALS AND THEIR WISDOM, 2002, O-SI-YO Truthart Publisher, $13.95. Traditional and personal philosophies with 20 of Susan's painting illustrations.

THE PHILOSPHY OF NATIVE AMERICAN CIRCLES, 2005, O-SI-YO Truthart Publisher, signed and numbered 1st edition, 500 copies, $14.95. Susan's philosophies with 18 of her painting illustrations.

Susan Thomas Underwood travels the Native American art show circuit nationwide and sells her art and other products. She is also available for speaking engagement at the studio address above.

Epilogue

I was pleased to offer this epilogue with WALK WITH SPIRIT's 3rd edition in 2005, and we are including it in this 4th edition in 2007.

Many readers told me great and good things about how this book broadened their spiritual scope and improved their lives. I did receive some negative response, though I'm sure many were too polite to express such emotion. The worst of it was an accusation of authoring a sacrilegious book. I fail to recognize any such meaning in a book so filled with words of the Creator and living a life of balance. It is unfortunate that any teaching beyond the stead-fast beliefs of our European founders are interpreted as such. This prejudice is why Native teachings were oppressed in the 1800s, and are obviously still oppressed today.

In these teaching and others, emphasis is on The Eternal Good, as reflected in our Shawnee word "Weshemonito", the Great Good Spirit. Does evil exist? The longer I live, the more this truth nags at me.

The Eternal Good always pushes us forward into new experiences and circumstances which grow us into higher levels of spiritual awareness (the law of spiritual growth). Though it may seem that evil tempts us and sometimes prevails, overall growth is *always* towards our betterment.

When we travel into The Void (a period of questioning, emptiness), this is most often when our greatest leaps of faith occur. When we question is when we grow. When we do not question is when we stand steadfast in our righteousness and refuse to look beyond. Is the absence of The Eternal Good (God, if you will). . . . The void? Where does The Void take us?

A World Based On Opposites

Is there darkness, or an absence of light?
Do we perceive this absence of light as darkness, or is it simply a place where light is not?

Is an absence of truth a falsehood? Is the absence of abundance....lack, or the absence of calm....a storm? Hence, the greatest of all questions, "Is the absence of Good......evil? May we simply perceive that absence as evil?

These opposites seem to be inter-changeable, as one leads back to the other. We with our tiny minds can not understand The Great Mystery of the eternal inner-weaving of life's threads!

A Physical Example

Preparing an egg for painting, I was attempting to remove its liquid center. Using a hypodermic needle, I labored to suction *out* in order to pull *out* the mass. Try as I might, my actions were doomed.

I knew this could be done, as other egg painters were clearly successful in removing the centers of their eggs. Changing my thinking into a problem-solving mode, I decided to go into the other end and *push air in*. The liquid center flowed *out* of the hole I had made in the other end! I realized the law of opposites had prevailed in this situation, I had to push *in* in order to displace the insides *out*.

Th*e law of opposites* prevail in daily life. The Good Book says, "We must *give* in order to *receive*". Why can't it be, "We must get in order to receive"? Just as we must *save* money in order to *acquire* wealth, and *work hard* in order to *rest well*; in order to become happy, we must first experience discomfort, grief, and sadness.

I value all who follow my writings and art. Because of your support, I am able to allow the creative flow to continue and manifest through my products. May you *walk with spirit* and *be all that is* for you this time around!